FOOTBALL SUPERSTARS

POGBA

RULES

SIMON MUGFORD   DAN GREEN

CONTENTS

POGBA! POGBA!

Let's meet football superstar **Paul Pogba.**

Manchester United's

MAGIC MIDFIELDER

shot to fame as a teenager and has gone on to win titles including **Serie A,** the **Coppa Italia,** the **Europa League** and the ultimate football prize, the *WORLD CUP.*

SO, WHAT MAKES **POGBA** SUCH A GOOD PLAYER?

Power
Super strong, he dominates the midfield.

Energy
Capable of sudden bursts of speed and powerful movement.

Height
He towers over his opponents and is dangerous in the air.

Passing
Delivers pinpoint passes that can change the course of a game.

Dead ball king
Master of spectacular free kicks and penalties.

POGBA IN NUMBERS

LET'S LOOK AT THE NUMBERS THAT MAKE POGBA SO SPECIAL.

4 ...SERIE A wins

1 ...WORLD CUP win

1 ...EUROPA LEAGUE win

1 ...LEAGUE CUP win

1 ...GOLDEN BOY award

77 CAPS and

10 GOALS for France

Massive **£89** MILLION

transfer from Juventus to Manchester United

Over **43** MILLION

followers on Instagram!

POGBA I.D.

NAME: *Paul Labile Pogba*

NICKNAME: *Pogboom, Il Polpo Paul (Paul the Octopus), La Pioche (The Joker)*

DATE OF BIRTH: *15 March 1993*

PLACE OF BIRTH: *Lagny-sur-Marne, France*

HEIGHT: *1.91 m*

POSITION: *Midfielder*

CLUBS: *Manchester United (2009-12), Juventus, Manchester United (2016-)*

NATIONAL TEAM: *France*

LEFT OR RIGHT-FOOTED: *Both*

Paul Pogba was born in 1993 in **Lagny-sur-Marne,** a town just to the east of Paris in France. He grew up in the nearby suburb of **Roissy-en-Brie.**

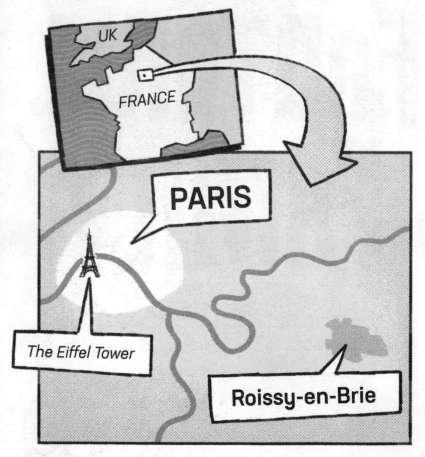

Paul lived with his mum, Yeo, and his older **twin brothers,** Mathias and Florentin.

Paul's dad, *Antoine,* lived nearby, too.

The Pogba family lived on an estate called **Renardière**. It could be a **tough place** to grow up, but they had lots of friends and were very **happy there**.

Little Paul

From the age of about three, Paul played football with his brothers on the estate's pitch.

HEY BOYS –
DINNER'S READY!
(Mum's voice)

BOP!

Paul's mum ALWAYS knew where to find them . . .

They were a **very competitive family!**
Paul and his brothers loved **playing sport**
and were always trying to outdo each other.

If they couldn't play football, they had
endless games of **table tennis.**

TEAM POGBA

Paul's dad, Antoine, had been a footballer and a coach in his home country of **Guinea.**

He trained Paul and his brothers when they played football in Renardière.

Mathias and Florentin grew up to be professional footballers, too.

20

Mathias and Florentin were born in Guinea and played for the national side.

In **1998,** when Paul was just five, France hosted the **World Cup.** Not only that, they beat **Brazil** in the final to become

WORLD CHAMPIONS!

Paul thought all of the French team were *AWESOME,* especially the midfielders, like:

Youri Djorkaeff

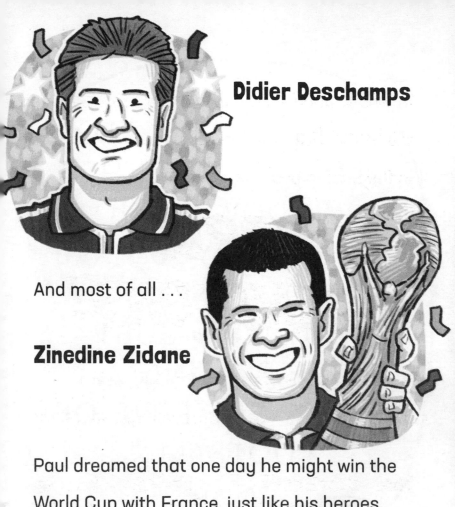

Didier Deschamps

And most of all . . .

Zinedine Zidane

Paul dreamed that one day he might win the World Cup with France, just like his heroes.

23

"MY MUM USED TO CALL OUT THE WINDOW: 'PAUL, COME ON, YOU HAVE SCHOOL TOMORROW.' BUT WE'D JUST KEEP PLAYING . . . THAT'S THE LOVE OF FOOTBALL."

Paul Pogba

24

CHAPTER 3

YOUNG STAR

At the age of **six,** Paul was already a **very skilful player.** He was brilliant at dribbling and ball control, and was an ace goalscorer, too.

Paul's dad taught him how and when to **pass** to his team-mates.

It was soon time for Paul to join his brothers at the **Roissy youth team**.

HE COULDN'T WAIT!

Paul quickly became Roissy's best player.

He was always at the centre of the action.

With Paul in the team, Roissy won

LOTS AND LOTS of matches!

One day, the coach challenged Paul to do
150 keepy-uppies.

Two days later, Paul came back and did it:

50 with his **right foot**

50 with his **left foot**

and 50 with his **head!**

Paul had lots of friends at Roissy. He loved being the **star of the show** and entertained everyone with **silly dances** and **funny jokes.**

Paul's new hero was **Ronaldinho,** who played for **Paris Saint-Germain** at the time.

WHOMP!

He loved copying the Brazilian star's *cool tricks* and *slick moves.*

Paul **lived for football.** When he wasn't training with Roissy, he'd be playing with his friends back in **Renardière.**

He was ready for a new challenge, but Paul and his family wanted to take it one step at a time.

When he was 13, Paul joined **Torcy.**
This local youth team played
at a higher level.

Scouts from big French clubs like

Paris Saint-Germain and **Lyon**

had all heard about Paul.

But in **2007,** when he was 14, Paul joined the academy at **Le Havre.** They played in the second division, but it was a fantastic club for a young player.

And it wasn't too far to come home and see his mum!

Le Havre is the oldest football club in France.

Sometimes, Paul needed to **focus on his game** and work harder.

The coaches had to give him a telling off!

38

But in his **second season,** Paul was made captain of the **under-16s.** He was becoming a star midfielder and proving himself to be a natural leader.

Paul's team beat some of the top sides in the **under-16 league,** such as **Lyon** and **Nancy.**

Paul was the **star player** at Le Havre.

He quickly became known as one of the **best young players** in Europe.

Lots of really **big clubs** wanted to sign Paul.

But where would he go next?

40

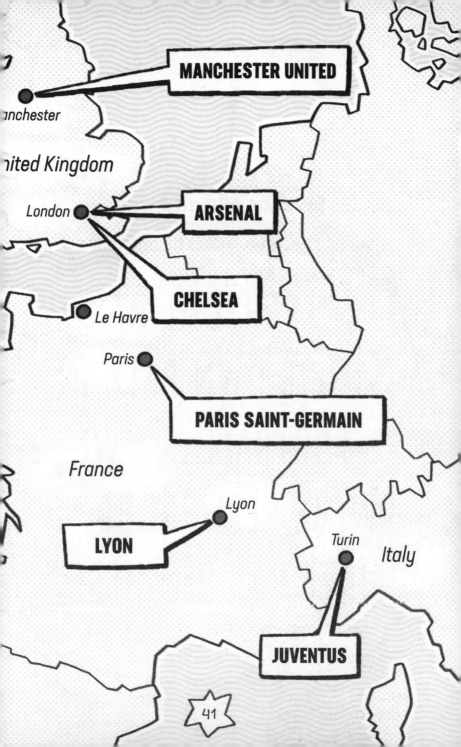

"EVERYONE HAS THEIR OWN PATH IN FOOTBALL . . . WE WERE VERY PROUD TO HAVE HAD HIM HERE."

Michael Lebaillif, Paul's coach at Le Havre

CELEBRATION TIME

A great goal deserves a **great celebration** - and Pogba's are some of the **best** in the business.

He has a whole range of crazy **dance moves** and **cool poses** for the fans!

Best of all, there's the **Dab dance** that he did with Jesse Lingard:

Paul has 'retired' the Dab now!

THE DAN DAD DANCE
(should be retired!)

45

Paul's **hairstyles** are always cool, often crazy, and **never boring.**

WHICH ONE IS YOUR FAVOURITE?

Mohawk

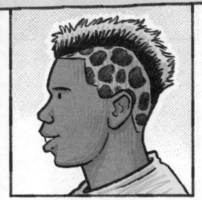

Leopard

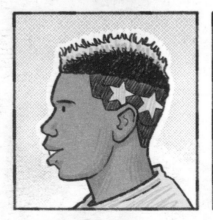

Stars

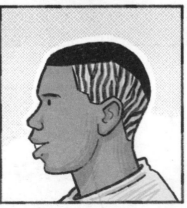

Stripes

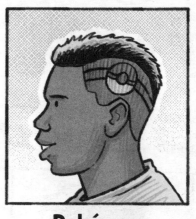

Pokémon

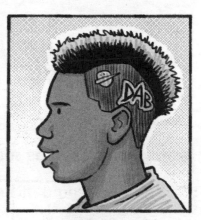

Dab

Pogboom

47

MONEY MAN

According to *Forbes* magazine, Pogba was the 50th highest-paid athlete in the world in 2020.

He earns around

£15 MILLION

a year at Manchester United.

"WHEN I SAY I WANT TO BECOME A LEGEND . . . FOR ME, IT'S A CHALLENGE. MY DESIRE, A DREAM. I'M NOT SAYING I'LL GET THERE, BUT IT'S WHAT I WANT."

Paul Pogba

CHAPTER 6

WORLD CLASS

CAPTAIN BLUE

With Paul starring as the **under-16s captain** for Le Havre, he soon found his way into the **French national team.**

Paul played at every youth level from **under-16** to **under-20** and was the regular captain.

IT WAS AN INCREDIBLE HONOUR!

U-20 WORLD CUP

France qualified for the **2013 Under-20 World Cup** in Turkey - and Paul was the captain!

The team met **Uruguay** in the final, which ended in a **penalty shoot-out**.

Paul scored the first penalty. He took lots of **little steps** before he struck the ball. It was very cheeky - just like Paul!

France scored three more penalties and

Paul was a

WORLD CHAMPION!

Paul won the **Golden Ball** as best player of the tournament.

WORLD CUP 2014

Paul played his first senior game for France in a **2014 World Cup Qualifier** against Georgia.

France qualified – and Paul was in a squad that included super strikers . . .

. . . **Karim Benzema**

56

... **Antoine Griezmann**

... and **Olivier Giroud**.

WOW!

Paul scored in the knockout game against **Nigeria**.

He was also named *Best Young Player* of the Tournament.

57

EURO 2016

Paul was in the squad for **EURO 2016**, which was being held in **France.**

After a couple of bad games, Paul put in an awesome performance against **Iceland** (who had knocked England out in the Round of 16.).

France beat world champions **Germany** to reach the final in Paris. *AMAZING!*

In the end, France lost the final 1-0 to **Cristiano Ronaldo's side, Portugal.**

WORLD CUP 2018

15 JULY 2018

WORLD CUP FINAL

LUZHNIKI STADIUM, MOSCOW

FRANCE 4-2 CROATIA

France were the **hot favourites** to win the final.

They were **2–1** up when **Paul** scored his **only goal** of the tournament. What a time to score!

BOFF!

20 years earlier, Paul and his brothers had watched France win the world cup on TV.

FRENCH LEGENDS

Paul is one of **FIVE** French players to score in a World Cup final. Here are the other four members of this special club!

Antoine Griezmann
The Barcelona ace striker scored to regain France's lead in 2018.

Kylian Mbappé
PSG's superstar scored the fourth goal in 2018, aged just 19.

Zinedine Zidane
This midfield genius scored twice in 1998 and once in 2006.

Paul's childhood hero.

Emmanuel Petit
Former Arsenal and Chelsea midfielder - scored the third goal in 1998.

Pogba was the **first Manchester United** player to **score** in a **World Cup final.**

63

PAUL'S FRANCE RECORD

CAPS	GOALS	ASSISTS
77	10	8

"TONIGHT, I WANT US TO BE IN THE MEMORY OF ALL THE FRENCH PEOPLE WHO ARE WATCHING US."

Paul, speaking in the dressing room before the 2018 World Cup final.

2009 was a **BIG** year for Paul. That summer, aged just 16, he left Le Havre – and France – to join the **academy** at one of the biggest clubs in the world:

MANCHESTER UNITED

Old Trafford,
Manchester United
home ground.

Paul did what he always did when he joined a new team:

He **amazed** everyone with his skills . . .

BOP!

Scored some **awesome** goals . . .

WAP!

Laughed, danced and **made new friends.**

This is when Paul met *Jesse Lingard.*

In 2011, Paul won his first trophy at United. The **under-18s** beat Sheffield United to win the **FA Youth Cup.**

At the time, the Manchester United squad included some of the **best players** ever to wear the famous United shirt.

Star striker
Wayne Rooney . . .

Wing wizard
Ryan Giggs . . .

Cool centre-back
Rio Ferdinand . . .

And midfield master
Paul Scholes.

Would Paul ever get his

chance in the first team?

In the **2011–12** season, Paul made his **first–team debut,** but then he spent most of the time on the bench.

Sir Alex Ferguson, the team manager, told him to be patient. But Paul couldn't wait. It was time for his next move.

CHAPTER 8

ITALIAN GOLD

After **three years** at Manchester United, Paul was on the move again. He joined the **GIANTS** of Italian football, **Juventus**, at the age of 19.

The Turin side had just been crowned **Serie A champions.** Paul would be playing alongside some of Italy's finest players, including . . .

Midfield mastermind **Andrea Pirlo . . .**

Rock solid centre-back
Giorgio Chiellini . . .

And goalkeeping legend
Gianluigi Buffon.

Soon after his debut, Paul became a first-team regular. He was playing in the **Champions League** and learning from the best.

IT WAS EVERYTHING HE HAD DREAMED OF.

Juventus were *Serie A champions* again and Paul had his first major trophy.

Paul played **37 games** and scored **five goals** in his first season.

POGBOOM!

It's near the end of the **first half** and the ball comes to Paul, who is almost out at the halfway line . . .

He half-volleys the ball: **POW!** It zooms, bends and bounces off the crossbar into net.

The Juventus fans called Paul *Il Polpo* (The Octopus) because of his long legs!

2013-14 HIGHLIGHTS

10 NOVEMBER 2013

SERIE A

JUVENTUS 3-0 NAPOLI

Paul scores another fantastic long-range goal – **POGBOOM!**

20 FEBRUARY 2014

EUROPA LEAGUE ROUND OF 32, 1ST LEG

JUVENTUS 2-0 TRABZONSPOR

Paul leaps to meet a cross from **Carlos Tevez** *late in* **injury-time** *to score his* **first goal** *in a European competition.*

It was during this season that Paul won the **Golden Boy** award. He was **OFFICIALLY** the best young player in Europe

Juventus won **Serie A** again!

2014-15 HIGHLIGHTS

4 NOVEMBER 2014

CHAMPIONS LEAGUE GROUP STAGE

JUVENTUS 3-2 OLYMPIAKOS

*Paul scores Juventus' third goal to win the match. It is his first **Champions League goal** and his **100th** game for Juventus.*

84

22 NOVEMBER 2014

SERIE A

LAZIO 0-3 JUVENTUS

*Paul scores **TWO brilliant goals** - one with his right foot and one with his left!*

6 JUNE 2015

CHAMPIONS LEAGUE FINAL

JUVENTUS 1-3 BARCELONA

*A disappointing result, but Paul's **first Champions League final** is also Juve's first in 12 years.*

At least they won
Serie A — again!

For what would be his **last season** at Juventus, Paul was handed the **Number 10 shirt.** This had previously been worn by Italian legends **Alessandro del Piero** and **Roberto Baggio.**

Alessandro del Piero

Roberto Baggio

Paul marked his **100th game** in Serie A in style, with a trademark long-range goal against local rivals Torino.

POGBOOOM!

Paul won a *FOURTH* Serie A title — of course!

POGBA'S JUVENTUS RECORD

SEASON	GAMES	GOALS	ASSISTS
2012-13	37	5	-
2013-14	51	9	16
2014-15	41	10	11
2015-16	49	10	13
TOTAL	178	34	40

Four Serie A titles in **four seasons!** It was a great record!

CHAPTER 9

#POGBACK

In 2016, the new Manchester United manager, **José Mourinho,** had money to spend.

So Pogba returned to United for an estimated

£89 MILLION!

#POGBACK

REUNITED

This was a **WORLD RECORD** signing at the time.

MY FIRST FOOTBALL FACTS

BALL

Also in the squad were legendary Swedish striker **Zlatan Ibrahimovic . . .**

And an 18-year-old **Marcus Rashford.**

Paul took a little while to settle in at his old club, but was soon **back on form.** He played an important part in helping United reach the final of the **Europa League.**

24 MAY 2017

EUROPA LEAGUE FINAL

AJAX 0-2 MANCHESTER UNITED

*Halfway through the first half, Paul gets the ball and fires with his left foot. The ball is deflected and **PING** - it's in the back of the net.*

POGBA WINS A MAJOR EUROPEAN TROPHY IN HIS FIRST SEASON!

#POGBACK

Paul was named Europa League **Player of the Season.**

2017-18

Paul started his **second season** back at United in brilliant form, scoring goals in the first **two** Premier League matches.

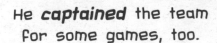

He *captained* the team for some games, too.

But then he got **injured** . . .

And some people said he

wasn't **good enough** . . .

DERBY DOUBLE

7 APRIL 2018

PREMIER LEAGUE

MANCHESTER CITY 2
MANCHESTER UNITED 3

United are **trailing 2–0** at half-time and look to be heading for defeat at the hands of their fierce rivals.

Guess who inspires the **fightback?**

POGBA
OF COURSE!

He scores **TWO GOALS IN TWO MINUTES** to get United back on terms - and ultimately win the game.

POGBA WAS **POGBACK** IN A DERBY CLASSIC.

Paul was named **Man of the Match** for his heroic display.

POGBA'S UNITED RECORD 2016-18

SEASON	GAMES	GOALS	ASSISTS
2016-17	51	9	6
2017-18	37	6	12

"IT WAS LIKE I'D JUST COME BACK HOME. I JUST WENT FOR A HOLIDAY."

Paul Pogba, on his return to United

CHAPTER 10

LE MAN UNITED

There were plenty of **HIGHS** and **LOWS** for Pogba in 2018-19.

He began the season wearing the **captain's armband . . .**

And scored from the spot in United's first matches in both the **Premier League** and **Champions League.**

But then he fell out with **José Mourinho** and spent time on the bench.

United's season was not going well.

José Mourinho was **fired** and replaced

by ex-United striker and fan favourite,

Ole Gunnar Solskjaer.

Paul welcomed Ole to the club by starting to score again.

POGBOOOM!

United began an unbeaten run of **12 GAMES** in the **Premier League,** during which Pogba racked up **EIGHT GOALS** and **SIX assists.**

Paul was back to his best - running the game, **scoring goals** and setting them up for his team-mates.

Football Superstars News

POGBA:
THE BEST MIDFIELDER IN THE WORLD?

Paul scored **16 gnals** this season, his highest tally for United!

2019-20 SEASON

This was another **rollercoaster season** for Paul Pogba.

There were **transfer rumours.**

POGBA TO MADRID

SPORT

JUVENTUS: WE WANT POG BACK

108

Then he got an **ankle injury.**

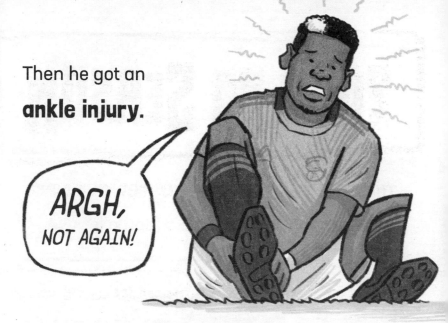

And then came the **Coronavirus** global pandemic.

2020-21 SEASON

With games being played in empty stadiums, it was a strange time to be a footballer.

But despite doubts about Pogba's future, and continuing injury problems, Paul was still **WORLD CLASS** when it mattered.

In **January 2021**, Paul scored an absolutely brilliant goal to win against **Fulham.** A long-range, left-footed **thunderbolt** which was classic Pogba.

Paul returned from injury in March and **scored** against **AC Milan,** sending United to the **Europa League quarter-finals!**

NUMBER 6

It is a **HUGE** honour for a player to wear the famous Manchester United shirt.

And Paul's **NUMBER 6** has been worn by some true Red Devils legends:

NOBBY STILES
1960-1971
Like Pogba, Stiles was a World Cup-winner – triumphing with England in 1966.

STEVE BRUCE
1987-1996

Bruce was a centre-back who scored loads of goals and won three league titles!

JAAP STAM
1998-2001

The rock solid centre-back was part of the famous Treble-winning team in 1999.

RIO FERDINAND
2002-2014

Six-times winner of the Premier League and one Champions League, Rio wore the number 6 in his first season.

POGBA'S UNITED RECORD 2019-21

SEASON	GAMES	GOALS	ASSISTS
2018-19	47	16	11
2019-20	22	1	4
2020-21	30	5	3

"I SCORED A COUPLE OF DECENT LEFT-FOOT GOALS IN MY DAY BUT NOT ONE THAT GOOD!"

Ole Gunnar Solskjaer on Pogba's goal against Fulham

CHAPTER 11

POGBA RULES!

AT AN ESTIMATED

£58 MILLION

Pogba is Manchester United's third-most valuable player.

	PLAYER	ESTIMATED VALUE
1	BRUNO FERNANDES	£81 MILLION
2	MARCUS RASHFORD	£72 MILLION
3	PAUL POGBA	£58 MILLION

And also the third-most valuable French player.

	PLAYER	ESTIMATED VALUE
1	KYLIAN MBAPPÉ	£162 MILLION
2	RAPHAËL VARANE	£63 MILLION
3	PAUL POGBA	£58 MILLION

Pogba always attracts attention,

on and off the pitch.

NEWS

POGBA RU

POGBA!

FOOTBALL

POGBA!

Whether it's a new **hairstyle,** a **goal celebration**, a **transfer rumour** or a

SIMPLY STUNNING PERFORMANCE.

BOOM!

POGBA RULES!

HONOURS AND RECORDS

A RUNDOWN OF POGBA'S BIG WINS

SERIE A
2012-13
2013-14
2014-15
2015-16

COPPA ITALIA
2014-15
2015-16

SUPERCOPPA ITALIA
2013
2015

EFL CUP
2016-17

EUROPA LEAGUE
2016-17

U-20 WORLD CUP
2013

QUIZ TIME!

How much do you know about **PAUL POGBA?** Try this quiz to find out, then test your friends!

1. Which year was Pogba born?

_____

2. Can you name one of Paul's brothers?

_____

3. Which other sport did Paul and his brothers like to play?

_____

4. What was the name of Paul's first club as a boy?

_____

5. Which side did Paul join when he was 14?

_____

6. Which team did Pogba score against in the 2018 World Cup Final?

---

7. How many goals did Paul score for Juventus?

---

8. How much did Manchester United pay Juventus for Paul in 2016?

---

9. Name one competition that Paul has won with Manchester United.

---

10. How many Manchester United managers has Pogba played for?

The answers are on the next page *but no peeking!*

ANSWERS

1. 1993

2. Mathias or Florentin

3. Table tennis

4. Roissy

5. Le Havre

6. Croatia

7. 34

8. £89 million

9. EFL Cup or Europa League

10. Three
(Sir Alex Ferguson,
José Mourinho,
Ole Gunnar Solksjaer)

PAUL POGBA:
WORDS YOU NEED TO KNOW

Premier League
The top football league in England (also called the Premiership).

EFL Cup
The second-tier English knockout cup competition.

Serie A
The top football league in Italy.

Champions League
European club competition held every year. The winner is the best team in Europe.

Europa League
The second-tier European club competition

Coppa Italia
Italian knockout cup competition

Supercoppa Italiana
Match between winners of the previous season's Serie A and the Coppa Italia.

ABOUT THE AUTHORS

Simon's first job was at the Science Museum, making paper aeroplanes and blowing bubbles big enough for your dad to stand in. Since then he's written all sorts of books about the stuff he likes, from dinosaurs and rockets, to llamas, loud music and of course, football. Simon has supported Ipswich Town since they won the FA Cup in 1978 (it's true - look it up) and once sat next to Rio Ferdinand on a train. He lives in Kent with his wife and daughter, a dog, cat and two tortoises.

Dan has drawn silly pictures since he could hold a crayon. Then he grew up and started making books about stuff like trucks, space, people's jobs, *Doctor Who* and *Star Wars*. Dan remembers Ipswich Town winning the FA Cup but he didn't watch it because he was too busy making a Viking ship out of brown paper. As a result, he knows more about Vikings than football. Dan lives in Suffolk with his wife, son, daughter and a dog that takes him for very long walks.